I0756302

FINISHING LINE PRESS
www.finishinglinepress.com

Bronxville

poems by

Lee Stockdale

Finishing Line Press
Georgetown, Kentucky

Bronxville

For Gail
Of course

Home is the place where, when you have to go there,
They have to take you in.
Robert Frost, *The Death of the Hired Man*

ISBN 979-8-89990-333-5 First Edition

ACKNOWLEDGMENTS

I am grateful to the following publications where versions of these poems first appeared:

Atlanta Review, "Levee"
myhometownbronxville.com, "Bronxville"
Poetry Review, "My Dead Father's General Store in the Middle of a Desert"
storySouth, "Moving Sidewalk"
The Prose Poem, "Peacocks"
United Kingdom Poetry Society, video broadcast, "French Resistance"
Whitefish Review, "Depression Bus"

Publisher: Leah Huete de Maines
Editor: Christen Kincaid
Cover Art and Design: Phil Heffernan / Lou Servidio-Morales
Author Photo: Vera Miljković, Vera Miljković Studio, New York, NY

Order online: www.finishinglinepress.com
also available on amazon.com

Author inquiries and mail orders:
Finishing Line Press
PO Box 1626
Georgetown, Kentucky 40324
USA

Contents

PART ONE: THE SUBWAY DOESN'T STOP HERE ANYMORE

My Dead Father's General Store in the Middle of a Desert

It has gas pumps with red horses and wings,
but is not merely a gas station, your father is not my father,
standing over me with a clipboard, checking off things done and left
undone.

He seems happy at this last stop before death for those living,
before life for those not yet born,
where his general store deals in flour, sugar, pieces of hacked meat,
or liver, reddish purple, a heart he wraps in brown paper.
He cuts my hair beneath the tin awning. I must have gotten here
from one direction or other on the road that stretches horizon to horizon,
the desert heat shimmering my eyes into pools.

I crawled in on my hands and knees,
he handed me an ice-cold orange Nehi drink.
It's pure coincidence that this store is my father's.
I ask him where all this stuff comes from, as no trucks travel this road
to replenish merchandise no one buys.
He doesn't like questions that challenge his existence.
I become quiet, he's cutting my hair
and might consciously or unconsciously make me look bad.

You're doing a great job out here, I say, which he knows is bullshit—
how many fathers, even if they are dead, set up a general store in a desert.
I persist, *You keep the shelves stocked, floor broomed, bathroom clean.*
The more I talk, the more I encourage myself to love him for the trouble
he went to
making all this seem real, with cans of various sized nails, beans, rice,
shelves of liquor, deli section with giant pickles.

I begin to see what a dear, sweet man he is. Is this because he is dead?
I wish he were alive again.
I don't think he killed himself to be mean to me personally.

At night, he says, *howling coyotes come down from the mountains*
and leave notes, Bible verses, threatening messages, love letters.
Everything a coyote wants to get off its chest.
I ask if they come every night.
He says, *Without fail.*

Bronxville

Bronxville city of magnificent possibilities
Bronxville university of fabulous mentors
Bronxville of choruses of choirs
Bronxville from early morning until late at night
Bronxville where dreams are dreamed and come true
Bronxville hive of intellectual bees
Bronxville workshop for literature and drama
Bronxville teeming with art and experiment
Bronxville with manifold unexplored doorways and corridors
Bronxville painters with easels of paint
Bronxville love on all horizons
Bronxville auditioning players for the play
Bronxville there is always work to be done
Bronxville every sky is the limit
Bronxville imagination resourcefulness given full rein
Bronxville where you fly without wings

Blue Star

On the train from Miami to North Carolina,
different cars for different summer camps.
Camp Blue Star for just Jewish kids
makes me feel strange,
I go to elementary school with these kids.

My father died.
We move to a town with no Jews at all.
My new stepfather makes casual jokes about Jews.
He calls them “Hebes,”
their cars “Jew canoes,”
Blacks are “Boogies,”
Italians—“Wops.”
A real estate broker, he won’t sell a house
to a Jewish family.

I hate my stepfather and call him *Fat Frog*.
I hate that town,
but today wear a Broncos alumni hoodie,
embracing my inner Bronxville.
My high school reunion is coming up,
I’ll go,
still trying to clean up my ugly past.

First Day of School in a New Town

The week before, I was in sunny South Florida,
today I'm freezing in a foreign country,
Switzerland, maybe, with all the snow, since
we had to move in the middle of January,
where I stomp my feet in new rubber boots
at the city bus stop after school.

Here it comes,
I have never been happier,
and off we go up Pondfield Road.

After a while, we are so far from Bronxville,
I get off the bus to find a pay phone,
and tell my mother, *I'm in Mount Vernon.*

Her voice is so angry I could have just killed a man.
Mount Vernon! Where in the world is Mount Vernon?
    I don't know where Mount Vernon is,
    but I got the wrong bus and that's where I am.
Oh, for God's sake, I'll come get you.

I tell her the drug store I'll be standing in front of,
and there she is with her diamond-cut eyes
burning a hole in my ineptitude.

Best Friends

In Miami, I had a best friend,
when we moved, he might as well have died.
Bronxville boys already had best friends,
I couldn't be one, I got there too late.

John was new, too, so—*Let's be best friends.*
John was more worldly, he'd moved from The City
where he'd been a member of Knickerbocker Greys,
some kind of special Boy Scouts.

John went to Columbia and studied Chaucer.
I went to a State school and joined the Army.
Fifty years later, we are still best friends,
John **Likes** whatever I post online,

if it's a poem he comments, "Terrific! Fantastic!"
That's what best friends are for,
if one posts a poem,
the other says, "Terrific! Fantastic!"

The Subway Doesn't Stop Here Anymore

It's only an illogical internal pressure
that makes me believe I should do anything at all
the face of a clock with eyes and a mouth
hands that spin from the nose in the middle
like the earth itself, nosing around
ping-ponging planets out of the way
through some God force emanating from the 2nd Avenue train
flying riders' hair like newspaper pages
circling the globe, the oceans, the city
to the truck I drive for the Bethlehem Bakery
calling me to the new resurrection
what's wrong with the old one
I don't see angels—I read about them
maybe they'd like a croissant and some coffee
as they send back reports from the forty-day desert
who was it there and what did He leave us
backpacking America in hiking sandals
Johnny Appleseed seeding, receding
I recall nothing of what I learned in school
historic dates, algebraic equations
Percy Bysshe Shelley, dissecting a worm
air raid dancers, eucalyptus trees
mangoes, cantaloupes, fruit with no names
passed between hands in the Jordan River
count the drops of rain as they fall
who can count them and not go mad
you know it exists, this exhaustive list
we are like the forgotten angels
puppets on strings slid through God's fingers for fun
singing the song of hair-flying subways
my feet are shivering, I need dry socks
and eyes in the palms of my hands to keep watch
for whether this subway's coming or not
if it doesn't that shouldn't change anyone's plans
but that's what love does, it makes you go bonkers
we must love one another from Bronxville to Yonkers.

Pepper & Salt

My mother used to write poetry
until my father killed himself.

When she remarried,
we moved to New York,

where she submitted ditties
to *The Wall Street Journal,*

and would tell us she had
"a little something"

in the *Pepper & Salt* section.
These "little somethings,"

about eight lines max,
made me sad for her

masking the pain
her real poetry would expose,

that people in Bronxville
would see and understand.

Depression Bus

The Bronxville Town Council allocated funds to repurpose
a school bus for depression, painted leftover Day-Glo orange
from the previous summer's Depression Fair.
The bus pulls into your neighborhood, you get on
and there are things to do: play solitaire, read old magazines, but

the Depression Bus "WILL NOT CURE YOUR DEPRESSION,"
expressly written on the poster with rules: "NO SMOKING/VAPING,"
"NO PROFANITY," "NO MUSIC." Naming the bus

was open to the public from April 1st to the end of May. "Happy Bus"
got the most votes, but "Happy Bus" exposed the Town to liability
if someone did not, in fact, get happy. In a cooler

are free juice boxes and vanilla cookies in cellophane wrappers.
The bus has a limit of twenty depressed people over the age of eighteen.
If you're under eighteen, I'm not sure where you go.

When I saw the Depression Bus, it depressed me,
so I thought—*I better get on.*
The driver, reading a paperback, said, *Make yourself at home.*

I was the only one on the Depression Bus,
which made me feel even more depressed.
The more no other depressed people got on,
the more depressed I got.
I brightened when I saw Pete: *Pete looks depressed. I'm sure he'll get on.*
I waved, but Pete pretended not to see.

Now and then, the bus driver laughed. I thought he was happy
about getting paid to park in neighborhoods and read paperbacks.
I asked what it was and he told me a title I'd never heard of.

It started to rain. Then stopped after a while.

The driver's laughter made me feel better.
He seemed like a naturally happy person.
I was no longer depressed and got off the bus.
If anyone asks, I will tell them the Town Council made a good investment.

Oh, Sister

After school I hang out
with other kids
at Marianne's house
with its large windows
overlooking the town
as the Beatles' *Revolver*
blares from the den.

Marianne plays field hockey
in a plaid wool skirt.
My greatest reward
is making her laugh.

On one of those Fridays
as evening comes on
I'm alone with Marianne
upstairs in her bedroom
when she turns her back
and takes off her shirt
to change into something new
for the night
leaving me staring
at her bra strap
curved waist
and thick blonde hair.

She explains over a shoulder
her lack of self-consciousness—
You have sisters.
At that moment,
I wished I didn't.

Bugatti

More mystical than the movie itself,
that night John and I came from the Bronxville Theater
after watching Vanessa Redgrave in *The Loves*
of Isadora. At the end, she's strangled
by her scarf that gets tangled around the rear wheel
of a Bugatti,
driven by the—until then—unmet man
she loved from a distance and called *Bugatti.*

John and I loiter the silent streets
bathed yellow by street lamps
bugs bump against,
eerily quiet,
we want so much more,
even police we'd welcome,
although we're on acid.
We pretend toward minor mayhem,
philosophically discuss our disconnectedness,
blood brothers without the shedding of blood.

Now we are old men
in other boys' glances,
on their way to being us,
on our way to being them.

French Resistance

These private clubs are all the same, they make you crawl
through the HVAC system, where seniority rats shine flashlights in
your eyes, to assess whether you are condescending enough.

I give the password they just told me to use,
but they tell me, "It's wrong. You have to leave."
So I'll probably never see my sister again.
When there she is and—God—she looks great, her smart black dress
complementing her tightly wound hair, like she herself somewhat
tightly wound.
She acts like I'm a stranger, or a long-lost acquaintance,
I have to remind her, "We have the same parents."
She must recognize me—she corrects me: "*Had*."
"Well, yes, then you know me. We 'had' the same parents."

She acts blasé, like I'm a dog, as she places a fake diamond leash
around my neck and walks me along the wide boulevard
where people stroll wearing the latest fashions.
"Is this," I ask, "the Champs Elysée,
often prominently featured in foreign films?"
We sit in the sun at a sidewalk café
where the waiter serves me champagne in a bowl
as I gaze at the beautifully coifed French poodles,
all of whom, I intuit, play classical piano.

"Why," I ask, "do you belong to that club? It's so stuck up.
You were always more basic and down-to-earth."
"Come see, come saw," she says—I think that's French.

We saw back and forth with a two-man saw in the forest of the
French Resistance.
Sweat pours off her body and I'm amazed at the muscles
her lumberjack clothes can't hide. We drag logs to the sawmill
where Resistance fighters know and embrace her.

"You're not a dog
and you never were. You're my brother, I love you, but we must
be careful about whom we talk to.
They're everywhere, all over, spies against love,
spiritual Nazis out to kill hearts.
We'll make a bench from the wood they cut,
then sit here and talk, like a real sister and brother."

Through a Store Window

Eager to get inside the store
I park my car in the empty lot.
Why is it empty?
Is the store closed?

It's a Monday morning.
It shouldn't be closed.
I get out of the car
and walk toward the door.

Through the window
I see people inside,
opening boxes,
stocking shelves.

And, look—it's Bernie!
My old boss,
who died from a heart attack
after his run.

Bernie sees me,
and I can tell from his eyes,
he's asking, *Do you really*
want to come inside?

I back away,
as only now do I see
I am witnessing
the diligent work of the dead.

Dead Poets' Graves

Poets love visiting dead poets' graves.
Often the spirit of the dead poet will rise
and offer advice to the living poet
to stay away from dead poets' graves.

The poet is confident
the dead poet would be pleased
to see him standing over the grave,
as the poet feels a special connection,
which the dead poet does not,
since the poet is dead.

The poet tries hard to commune with the Spirit,
view the world through Walt Whitman's eyes,
stand beside him as he ministers to Civil War soldiers,
be Emily Dickinson stroking her cat,
be at least one strand of Emily's hair.

No one can know of the transmigration of souls
as the poet drives some useful object—
a pencil, a St. Patrick medallion, a buffalo head nickel—
into the dirt at the foot of the grave.

Levee

My friend told me she'd gone to the same levee
on the Mississippi that broke
when my father was a boy,
washing away the new house
his father built for the family,
causing the father to drink himself to death,
leaving them destitute,
forcing my grandmother to move
with my father's two younger sisters
to Alabama.
But not with my father.
The Depression worsening,
Alabama kin could not also feed a growing boy.

I learned this decades later from Sara Nell,
one of those sisters who said all four cried
as my father pleaded with his mother not to leave—
he could work and make money, they wouldn't go hungry:

> *The car drove away*
> *with Ruth's and my faces*
> *pressed against the glass.*
> *Your father standing in the road*
> *getting smaller and smaller.*

My friend went to that same Greenville levee,
careful to park away from others,
thinking she might scare them screaming her grief
for the twin soul of her childhood,
whose death flooded her
like the Mississippi.

I Am and Am Not Chagall

An angel flock plays gold-colored trumpets,
the sky is blue, deep deep blue blue,
and falls from white clouds filled with yellow
stars. A man with a black beard
pushes a black wheelbarrow,
inside the wheelbarrow is a singing pig.
The man says the singing pig is mine
and has been mine since the beginning of time.
I don't have to be Chagall for this,
I can be me and still have a pig.

The roads lead off in many directions,
deeply rutted,
winding over blue hills,
since the sky that falls
covers all the earth,
though with a blue
distinct from the streams,
the streams from the rivers,
the rivers from seas,
and none of the buildings
are pock-marked by shellshock,
they must have negotiated a lasting peace,
but because of my memories
I know of the danger,
and begin painting angels
as fast as I can.

PART TWO: PURE PLEASURE

Hello, Stranger

You lived down the hall,
we exchanged *Hellos*,
I was sure in time we'd
get to know one another.

You moved too soon
and left your cat
who followed me
up and down the hall.
Hello, stranger,
so I called her *Stranger*.

We moved to Seattle,
then LA,
back East, up and down the Coast,
now with a wife,
three kids,
lots of schools.

Stranger adapted
to myriad occupations,
apartments, houses,
a litany of fellow
domesticated pets.

She died last night.
Such a sweet cat.
Sweet to the end.
I thought you should know.

Pure Pleasure

There is no such thing as pure pleasure,
some anxiety always goes with it.
Ovid

What was Ovid's problem? Of course anxiety-less pure pleasure
is achievable. It's too bad
he lived in an age before psychotherapy.

Even a week at a yoga retreat might have produced
some pure pleasure
minus the anxiety. Was Ovid good enough

to his wife?
Perhaps she was making his life miserable—
because *he was making her life miserable first!*

Anyway, who goes around saying stuff like that?
He must have thought he was singularly
wise. Really, he sounds anxious.

Thank You, Melissa

I canceled home delivery of the *Sunday Times*
with online chatbot Melissa who wrote: *I am sorry to hear this.*
Why are you canceling?
I typed: *Too much to read.*
She wrote: *Do you know you can pause delivery?*
Not interested. Please cancel subscription.
Melissa wrote: *You can also suspend.*

What's the difference between pause and suspend?
Suspend is longer.
What if I combine pause with suspend?
lol you have to pick one or the other.
The lol made me suspect Melissa was a live human being.
I pick pause. Pause me forever.
For forever you should suspend.

She explained that with a monthly upgrade
I could get podcasts, background interviews,
exclusive behind-the-scenes stories,
and *Home delivery will be added on free!!!*

Those three exclamation points were so spontaneous,
no way Melissa was a non-human chatbot,
but likely a single mother with a baby to feed,
a large dog to walk in difficult weather,
possibly a restraining order against an Ex.

Overwhelmed with compassion, I wrote, *OK sign me up!!!*
with three exclamation points to affirm our oneness,
and the joy of a man who, only minutes before,
was about to cancel home delivery.

One-Act Play

They get in my cab for a Broadway play,
the woman wears a white dress with sparkles.

He's unaware he's underdressed, and otherwise
generally unaware. She reads out loud actors'

previous roles from a playbill she holds
to the window for light. He responds with his guy trip

in July to fish trout: *If we don't get wasted and drown.*
I could save this couple a lot of trouble, turn and tell them,

You are not right for each other,
which I could do since we are three blocks from the theater,

traffic is dead-stopped, and we could easily engage
in a frank three-way discussion.

The cab is costing him. He says, *Let's get out and walk.*
I am wearing heels, she says, without looking up.

He will not talk anymore, he is watching the meter,
the thermometer of his head about to pop.

In the silence I write a one-act play.
It all takes place in the back of a cab.

Termites of Love

Dan, the young Episcopal priest I trust,
knowing both his parents committed suicide,
appears at *Yes! Restaurant* where I serve health food
and gives me the key to his church to rehearse
The Hollow Men he's asked me to read
to dovetail with a sermon he plans to preach.

Grace Church is dark, I turn on the lights,
termites are everywhere, tiny hard workers
with baby bat faces, eating the floor, pews,
altar cross, leaving in aisles mounds of sawdust
they roll into a ball and out the front door,
where, in the street, they fashion a carriage,
and imply to me *Hop in* without actually saying it.

We go to a war zone, they eat the tanks.
We go to the courthouse, they eat corrupt judges.
We go to corporations, they eat CEOs.
We go to The White House, they eat a President.

I am grateful to be with the termites of love,
but need to rehearse this poem for Dan.
They understand and take me back to the church
where the compromised floor has fallen into the basement.

I will always wonder whether that night
when the termites of love ate Dan's church,
had something to do with his hanging up his vestments,
becoming a photographer, and opening an art gallery.

Bronxville Train Station

It is no longer snowing, but still freezing out.
Nice of my mother to drive me to the station
to get back to the city after I spend the night.
Even nicer, she waits for the train in the warm car
while we listen to depressing Adult
Contemporary Music. "Do you mind

if I change it?" She waves her cigarette—
The radio's yours.
I find Fleetwood Mac and *Go Your Own Way*
which she seems to like,
or at least taps along on the steering wheel.

I tap on the armrest, though it's clear that
we're not tapping together: my future's uncertain,
hers I don't want to think about either,
married to a man who doesn't read books,
not as smart as she is, or as smart as my father.

The train comes,
I kiss her on the forehead,
get out of the car,
and we go our own ways.

Peacocks

The Polish Labor Service treats them like kings and queens, blue-green peacocks who wander this base and fan in front of a line of tanks, causing the tanker to pop out of his turret, yank off his headphones and yell, *Fucking move!* before inching his metal behemoth forward.

The tanker, again, halts in front of the peacock, who stares at, and tells him: *We are guests of the Polish Labor Service, humble men, gentle and kind, whose families were killed in the Nazi Holocaust, who keep this base tidy and, really: for what? For the grace of living like elderly orphans in barracks not as nice as for American GIs who'll transfer back to The World in a year to girlfriends and mamas and Chevrolets. Go ahead, run me over, so that back in Iowa, when you hold your sweetheart, she will feel a peacock's blood on your hands.*

The tanker's Captain jumps out of his jeep. They have deadlines to meet at Ramstein Air Base. The Captain waves to shoo it away, but the peacock will not move, and now it's joined by a sister peacock, who fans and preens and screams in the street.

Moving Sidewalk

My plane got in late
leaving me no time
to get from Concourse *A* to *D*
for my connecting flight.

The shuttle train was out of order
so I had to use the moving sidewalk
where I encountered a boy about five
walking in the opposite direction
from that which the sidewalk was moving in,
followed by his mother
who I thought would turn the boy around,
until she began walking with him
in the opposite direction.

They both looked so happy,
I turned around and began walking
in the opposite direction myself,
which made them smile,
when others began to see the fun,
or excitement,
or something new to be had,
by turning around
and walking in the opposite direction,

until everyone,
dozens of people with rolling bags,
turned around and began walking
what could be termed backwards,
and it no longer mattered
if I made my flight,
it was just so good
to be doing something with strangers
who all decided that you can't
have too much of a good thing.

Biscotti Day

The biscotti truck rings its bell in the neighborhood,
people fly out doors to stand in line
like obedient preschoolers.

No one talks in the biscotti line.
They move slowly forward, inch-by-inch,
worried, wondering:
Will there be enough biscotti for me?
Will it run out?
Will some kind of calamity intervene
before I get my biscotti?

One biscotti, says a man,
as if it is the most natural thing in the world,
as if every day is Biscotti Day,
and there is no reason to be especially grateful
as the earth on its axis toils and spins.

Once Upon a Time at Shakespeare in the Park

Actors in modern clothes move to Donna Summer disco
at Shakespeare in the Park's performance of *Hamlet.*
Five or six young people in the grass down left
burst out laughing after every line.

No one asks them to leave or be quiet.
Maybe they're stoned.
I don't think they are drunk.
Maybe this is how they show their support.
Maybe they are hostile to one of the players,
trying to make them forget their lines.

Leonardo DiCaprio uses a flamethrower on his killer
in the movie *Once Upon a Time in Hollywood.*
She writhes like a marshmallow on a stick
and I laugh till I get tears in my eyes when I watch it on TV.
My wife walks in and asks, *What is so funny?*
I mumble something, and can't explain.

Mother and Animal-Man

How is it my mother is so much in the picture,
she's been more than dead for 25 years. I can't
take a step but there she is
in that hat, green linen suit jacket,
and rectangle pin with silver filigree framing

a winged animal-man
fashioned with bits of colored enamel.
The animal-man's black beard is absurdly long,
which always made me think he was wise.

He steps out from the pin and walks beside her,
now as large as my mother, talking back and forth.

I can't hear what they say,
or I hear,
but they speak in an other-worldly language.

We are now in the aisles of CVS
where I search for a box of brand name bandages
that will not fall off when I take a shower
to cover the cut I got from my bike when the lace
from my sneaker
wound tight round the pedal
that rose up and sank its teeth in my shin.

I pick up a box and read the label.
They talk—a decision—some final agreement.
She looks at me and shakes her head. The wound,
she is telling me, will heal on its own.

I Dream I Am Accepted to Art School

I sit on the stoop of John's apartment building where the art classes are held, catty corner from Bronxville School, when Mae, a senior partner from my law firm shows up, with a young woman and a former Army officer I know, his black hair slicked back and shiny with product. Mae's blonde curls cover the sides of her face. She is energetic, focused on some task. Moving her house?

The Army officer and I walk up Pondfield Road behind Mae and the other woman. I ask if he is Mae's administrative assistant, whether he is being paid. *No*—he laughs—*I am not her assistant. We share ideas. I travel with her. She's incredibly cheap.* We watch Mae open the door to where they are staying—a brown-shingled split-level, down in the tooth. I see

where I need to go, and get there, entirely, through interiors of buildings, to a church courtyard from the 1800s, so excited about the art classes, I throw the four casters from the office chair into the grass. Realizing this may be disrespectful, I retrieve them through the wrought iron gate. I want to pray,

but the grass is wet, find a dry patch and get down on my knees. A monk in a brown cassock bends over and says: *War is afoot between Germany and Russia.* I ask if they have closed the roads to Berlin. *Yes. They've also closed Teufelsberg*, and he mentions three or four other towns to demonstrate the gravity. Sitting back on the steps of John's apartment, I watch eight or nine men in front of the Post Office. They have full, well-trimmed red beards, and are signing up to join the Army, since they all belong to the same quasi-military organization, chanting some nutty slogan over and over.

An Army General stands to my left, monitoring the recruiting process. I ask him for information. Or his analysis. *If you are going to study art,* he says, *you should be able to figure it out on your own.*

Posthumous Praise for My Stepfather

You were my stepfather for a mere six years, then died.
Only now do I discount our arguments regarding race,
the Bay of Pigs, the Kennedys. I was a bad stepson
and ask your forgiveness, admitting I lied

and did drive your car to smoke pot with John at Choate
unaware you recorded the odometer: *I was just driving*
a hundred-and-forty miles around Bronxville.
I also lied about the haircut money, which was obvious

it was such a bad job—a girlfriend scissored off
only a little, and without real trimmers no neck fuzz.
The barber told you, when you called to ask, *No, your stepson*
didn't come in today. I thought your checking up on me

was not playing fair. And, yes, it was I who threw out the toy gun
you hid under socks in your top dresser drawer,
which you planned to use to confront a burglar.
What if the burglar has a real gun? If you point a toy gun

at a burglar, the burglar is going to shoot first and kill you.
I may have possibly saved your life.
Forgetting the reasons we hated each other,
I am grateful

your real son and my older sister introduced
their newly widowed parents, who got married
so we moved from Miami to Bronxville, a train ride away
from the GREATEST CITY IN THE WORLD.

Thank you, also, for not putting me on the street.

SPECIAL THANKS

To Gail and our children Zachary, Sara, Noah, Ben, and Leah, all of whom, because of my crazy career, moved from place to place and school to school more times than they wanted. Thank you!

To my poetry friends, A. Van Jordan, Amy Peterson, Amy Turner, Andrew Clark, Anna Warrock, Anthony Ramstetter, Beth Weinstock, Billy Collins, Brian Koester, Caleb Beisert, Cathy Smith Bowers, Chris Haub, Chris Julian, David Riddle, Emily Pease, Greg Lobas, Janet Orselli, Jessica Jacobs, John Hall, Kathryn Temple, Kathy Ackerman, Keith Flynn, Lauren Myers-Hinkle, Lisa Krueger, Luke Hankins, Marianne Carruth, Mark Doty, Moriah Cohen, Mel Green, Melanie Bookout, Melinda McGee, Michael Foran, Michael Hettich, Mike McCue, Mildred Kiconco Barya, Mirande Bissell, Nancy Holmes, Nina Tovish, Pam Lippe, Pat Riviere-Seel, Patricia Smith, Phil Heffernan, Phil White, Philip Terman, Robert Ard, Scott White, Sherona Varulkar, Stephen "Stevo My Bevo" Barber, Susan Ayres, Vera Miljković, and Yehoshua November.

Finally, tremendous thanks to Finishing Line Press for your hard work, professionalism, and grace in bringing *Bronxville* to light.

ABOUT THE AUTHOR

Lee Stockdale loved poetry before he could read when his poet mother created a 45 RPM record of poems for his first grade class and Stockdale couldn't get enough *Jabberwocky*. The close friendship with John F. Kennedy resulted in his father's appointment as Ambassador to Ireland, so Stockdale spent part of his childhood as an Irish schoolboy. Stockdale's father committed suicide ten days after the assassination. His mother remarried and the family moved to Bronxville, New York.

After graduating from the University of Washington, Stockdale joined the Army as a Private to serve his country and have something to write about. He completed his career as a Judge Advocate (JAG) Colonel. His law degree is from Case Western Reserve and his MFA is from Queens University.

Stockdale's previous collection, Gorilla, was published by *Main Street Rag* and awards include the United Kingdom National Poetry Prize, *Whitefish Review* Montana Prize for Humor, *Atlanta Review* International Merit Award, and Sidney Lanier Poetry Prize. His work has appeared in *Poetry Review, The Guardian, Ekphrastic Review*, anthologies, and other journals. The North Carolina Poetry Society has named him a Gilbert-Chappell Distinguished Poet.

Stockdale and his wife, a potter, live in Asheville, where they practice hot yoga and feed the wild turkeys.

www.ingramcontent.com/pod-product-compliance
Lightning Source LLC
LaVergne TN
LVHW090538110826
845146LV00003B/1171